P9-DDR-406

# LIVING THE LIFE!

# The World of ELVIS Tribute Artists

VERVE
EDITIONS

# In Patty Carroll's World Beyond Words
## by Andrei Codrescu

Me and my people we've been working for decades to try to understand the cults of Elvis and Dracula. My people, Romanian-European skeptics with Enlightenment roots, have a hard time understanding why Americans, the freest and richest people on earth, have fits of ecstasy and chills of religiosity when hearing or viewing the aforementioned icons. I'll dispense with Dracula for now, because he's mostly imaginary and centuries old, and I'll direct my baffled and disturbed vision toward the growing God-like figure of Elvis. In 1966 when I arrived in the U.S.A., Elvis was a Las Vegas caricature to my generation, symbolically irrelevant and physically grotesque. Our idols were long-haired and skinny and filled with angry metaphysical anguish. When Elvis died and the Sixties ended, the excessive kitschiness of the next decade demanded an antidote and Elvis made his comeback via the tabloids, taking his place among a pantheon of freaky manifestations, including UFOs and zombies, who were coming back from the dead at a staggering rate. The ironic purging continued into the Eighties, but the figure of Elvis detached itself from its freakoid peers and started gaining momentum and altitude. The ascendant Elvis figure rose high enough to penetrate the ivory floor (more like pressed woodchips by then) of academe in the mid-nineties. At that point, Elvis became a multi-layered, multi-tentacled cultural phenom that knew no bounds. Not only was Elvis suddenly the key that unlocked the mysteries of mid-century of America, but, it turns out, there were some people for whom he had never diminished or increased in stature. There were people for whom Elvis was God in the beginning, in the bad-movie middle, and in the overwight and sad end. There were people who measured the stages of their lives in Elvis, who remembered important history by the Elvis song contemporary to it, who led a life ritually marked by Elvian ceremonies.

I was an Elvis novice until I was invited to deliver the concluding remarks at the Second International Elvis Symposium at the Memphis College of Art, a gathering of pop-scholars, theologians, artists, and fanatics. The Symposium coincided with the annual anniversary of Elvis's death, an occasion hosted by the official governors of the Elvis legacy trust(s) connected to Graceland and in no way connected with the Elvis fringes represented at our conference. I traveled to Memphis in an airplane full of Australian Elvis fans of a certain age and, for the most part, of a certain girth, wearing a variety of Elvis T-shirts issued over the years. Two of them conversed with me at length about where they were and what they were doing upon the release of important Elvis songs. One of them, a grandmother in her late sixties, claimed that on hearing "It's Alright, Mama," she had to get married the next day. Those were the days. The scholars and weirdos gathered under the huge blow-up rubber doll of Elvis in front of the Memphis College of Art, taught me many things. I had been aware for some time of the cabalistic significations of the name "Elvis": "lives," "lives," "evils," but not quite tuned in to the depth of occult tales they spun, or the depth of mystical feeling attached to them. Due to my singular job of delivering the "concluding remarks," I had to listen to everything, including vastly boring academic lectures and, more amusingly, the speculations of a former Secret Service guard for Richard Nixon who believed (with slides and clippings) that his boss had assassinated The King. From this seemingly endless quagmire of paranoid academic and popular suppurations there were only two ways out: suicide and Patty Carroll.

The fact that Patty appeared at just the right time is a miracle I attribute entirely to Elvis. I knew of Patty's work, I admired her photographs, but I had no idea that she would visit the conference for the purpose, it turns out, of saving my life. Patty had brought her camera, as she had for a long time, to photograph Elvis impersonators, many of whom were her friends. When she invited me along, I had no idea that she was an insider of the annual Elvis Impersonators' Ball and that she had had a long and abiding interest in the people who became Elvis every year. Some of them were Elvis all year and some of them were hoping, no doubt, to impersonate Elvis post-mortem. What would the ghost of Elvis make of of people squeezed into his suits mobbing the pearly gates I cannot imagine. On the other hand, death was not an issue: for the world-wide Elvi come to Memphis to be Elvis, life eternal was already theirs. Anyway, going backstage with Patty was like being allowed into the world's most exclusive club with Mick Jagger, or The King Himself. Elvi of every description greeted her with hugs and salutations. Patty and Patty's camera were surely something in this world, something beloved, something like Blue Suede Shoes, if such a thing can be. How else explain the adoration of child Elvi (whom she had seen grow up and whose parents she knew), Japanese Elvi, female Elvi, and even wheelchair-bound, handicapped Elvi? Patti knew them and had photographed them and had listened to their stories. They were her community, they trusted her, and they were going to do their best on stage because she was there. After my privileged visit backstage, I sat in the audience while Patty did her camera thing. The spectacle was amazing: each Elvis had fans. The younger Elvis had fans, the older Elvis had fans, and so did every other kind of Elvis, including the lesbian and the Japanese Elvis. It was as if every community on earth, including sexual subcultures and foreign countries, had sent their ambassadors to present their version of The King. It was a competition in the best sense of the word: spectators wept, sweat-soaked handkerchiefs were snapped up in awe by outraised hands, people fainted, spoke in tongues, had fits and orgasms. Had Elvis himself appeared during this orgy of Elvis-spirit he would have ranked but tenth or eleventh. I needed about five beers to feel the Spirit, but when I did I understood something profound: the Elvis impersonator community was religious but unlike any other religion. The people who worshipped The King did so by taking turns being Him. Other churchgoers are possessed by their respective divinities, but few, if any, have had the joy of anything as moving as performing frankly sexual Elvis songs for their liturgy. Patty's photos of these singularly inspired devotees constitute a sacred text of their own. You can go into each picture and hear stories or, if you're not up to it, you can just lower yourself into the faces herein and hear the passionate call of the Beyond.

My "concluding remarks" at the Second International Elvis Coonference were highly colored by the humanity of Patty's camera. The Nixon guy made no impression. Now that he book is here, I'll start working on getting my people to understand. About Dracula: Patty, are you interested?

# It's all about transformation

## by Patty Carroll

*Elvis* — a name so unusual that it has become an icon in itself. Even Elvis, the man, had trouble living up to Elvis, the persona, that he created out of himself. Like cells splitting, we now have thousands of versions of Elvis, the persona, living, singing, acting, and becoming "Elvis Tribute Artists." They have been called impersonators, impressionists, stylists, performers, interpreters, and many other names, but they all have one thing in common; they love Elvis, whoever he is in their hearts.

It is all about transformation. Elvis made himself into a showman, with the help of "The Colonel," a word of advice about clothing from Liberace, the support of his fans, and particularly in his own Elvis-unique, flamboyant style. Elvis set the bar for later rock and roll extravagant productions, concerts, music videos and the entire culture/industry that it has become. The first music videos were his movies, the first gyrations were from his hips, the first gaudy outfits were his own, the first elaborate stage shows were ritualized by him. While the world of rock and roll has splintered itself into it's own variations of hard rock, hip hop, rap, oldies, etc., the fans of the original man and his style of music continue to etch the indelible mark of Elvis in a variety of ways. The most prominent and visible incarnation of Elvis fandom is the plethora of Elvis Tribute Artists also known as ETAs, who also experience transformation. They become something new, a hybrid person; a new persona mixing Elvisness into themselves.

Each ETA works very hard to master the voice, the range of moves, the gestures, the subtle inflections, the overt costuming, the stage presence, the hair, a sense of humor and so many more aspects of unique Elvis traits that they cannot be totally described. But many ETAs do talk about the change that occurs when they ritually adopt the persona; starting with getting dressed, fixing their hair, and practicing the music. "Like Superman, you feel the power when you put on the jumpsuit." (Rick Marino) So then something indescribable happens; the guy who normally takes his kids to school, or goes to a 9-5 job, or leads some sort of ordinary life, becomes more than himself. He doesn't become Elvis or himself, but more of a variation on a theme of both. He is not one or the other, but like "fusion" food, he is a new flavor borrowed from several sources; satisfying and appealing in his own way. That combination is exactly what distinguishes one ETA from another. The unique blending of personality and talent, voice and movement, look and sound is what spur competitions for the "best."

The transformation provides both an illusion as well as a new reality. Fans make the leap over the person singing, into Elvis, to experience the suspension of disbelief and get lost in the memory of Elvis. Conversely, other fans fall equally in love with the actual ETA, who has his own stage presence and voice. He may don the clothes and style, but he maintains his own individuality. The quality of "Tribute" becomes the dividing point between the professional ETA and the amateur. So many people have the same dream, the same love, the same urge to be part of Elvis and his world, that they almost can't help themselves from trying it out. It is said that imitation is the sincerest form of flattery. In this case, the flattery can also lead to mockery and humiliation if the ETA has not practiced enough, or for some reason cannot maintain the illusion. Connoisseurship exists in all things, including subcategories of subcultures.

Elvis was not Hispanic, Asian, black, small, female, disabled, a midget, nor did he have any unusual outward traits. However, the ETAs come in every shape, color, nationality, age, sex, and disposition, without regard for the original person. Yet, Elvisness transcends all of these outward barriers. It is the inner life of the ETA that is important. Inside he (or she) has a connection with Elvis that is spiritual, emotional, or undisclosed. Elvis continues to get under the skin of his fans in a very genuine way. In fact, that is what prompted this project in the first place. Photographers can only actually show the exterior of a person in a picture. Yet, many portrait photographers work very hard to reveal the "soul" of their sitters, as if it were possible. I photographed each of these people's inner life, while simultaneously portraying their very visible, professional stage personae.

The ETAs exhibit their soulful selves every time they perform. They also bring joy, hope, and rejuvenation to people who share a connection with Elvis. They jumpstart memories of a different life, perhaps of a youthful time when Elvis was in his prime, or when life was simpler, easier, or just more fun. The ETAs are the embodiment of a dream, a fantasy of an illusion. That illusion is a search for Elvis himself. Each fan has an idea of Elvis. Each fan has a dream of Elvis. Each fan has a longing for Elvis. The ETA becomes the embodiment of that fantasy.

I hope you will enjoy the photographs, but mostly I hope you will enjoy who these people are, and what they mean in the world. We all have our fantasy lives, and are fans of someone, or love something. These people are not just about Elvis, who did live out his own American dream, but are about dreams themselves. To live without a dream is not to live.

# Mike Albert

"Ultimate Tribute"

Mike Albert looks, acts, sings, and almost becomes Elvis when he is on stage. He has an uncanny resemblance to him, and an incredibly strong voice. He has traveled the world with his musicians, "The Big E Band."

Performing for over 20 years

**DAY JOB:** Entertainer and auctioneer

**HOME BASE:** Columbus, Ohio

# Peter Alden

## "The Spirit of Elvis"

Peter Alden has had an artificial hip since he was three; this was an innovative implant with a hip that was to grow with him as he aged. When you see him wiggling and jiggling on stage it is hard to believe that he's been through such treatments. In high school Peter entered a talent contest and decided to don a silky pink shirt and perform an Elvis tune. He was a hit and thought maybe his interest in Elvis could become a part of his desire to become an entertainer. A coup for Peter is that his musical director and drummer in his band is David Fontana, the son of DJ Fontana.

*Performing for over 10 years*

DAY JOB: Substitute Teacher HOME BASE: St. Cloud, Florida

# Justin Shandor

"I'm kind of a shy guy. I love Elvis. I love Elvis music. I love Elvis' style. My wife even looks like Priscilla! His voice and memory will live on in all of our kids and grandkids."

Performing for over 5 years

**DAY JOB:** Elvis Tribute Artist
**HOME BASE:** Las Vegas, Nevada

# Junior Talley

## "Illusions of Elvis"

"I appreciate the fact that I can go out there and perform and keep the minds of the people in the audience off their jobs and let them think about Elvis."

Performing for over 12 years

**DAY JOB:** Elvis Tribute Artist

**HOME BASE:** Monmouth, Illinois

# Gene Capaul

## "King Karaoke"

"People are a lot easier to start a conversation with when I'm in costume. People pay attention while I'm in costume. It's like I have special control over them. Impersonation is the highest form of a compliment. I love the music and the man. He did what everyone dreams of doing."

*Performing for over 17 years*

**DAY JOB:** State Trooper

**HOME BASE:** Olivia, Minnesota

# Johnny Baron

## "Reflections of Elvis"

*Performing for over 16 years*
DAY JOB: **Elvis Tribute Artist**
HOME BASE: **San Francisco, California**

# Steve Sogura

"Memories of Elvis"

"I can't imagine where I'd be without the influence of Elvis Presley's music on my life."

Performing for over 14 years

**DAY JOB:** Elvis Tribute Artist
**HOME BASE:** Ravensdale, Washington

# Michael Hoover

## "Memories of Elvis"

"Being an ETA is my hobby and a job. Sometimes, though, I would just like to get away, out of the mold. Almost daily someone will come up to me and ask, 'Do you know who you look like?' And sometimes I just get a kick out of saying, 'Who, Ricky Nelson?'"

*Performing for over 20 years*

**DAY JOB:** Elvis Tribute Artist  **HOME BASE:** Garrisonville, Virginia

# Shawn Barry

"That's The Way It Was"

"Whenever I come on stage, I always hear them say, 'What a dreamboat.'"

**DAY JOB:** Elvis Tribute Artist
**HOME BASE:** Ottowa, Ontario, Canada

# Donny Edwards

## "King of Memories"

"Once I got past the stage fright, I started visualizing Elvis performing. I was just dropped into this life!"

*Performing for over 3 years*

**DAY JOB:** Elvis Tribute Artist
**HOME BASE:** Las Vegas, Nevada

# Rory Allen

## "Tribute to 'The King'"

"One of the best things I experience from doing this tribute show is seeing how the music touches people in a deeply personal way. One night I sang to a lady with MS who had a constant, involuntary trembling through her whole body. When I took her hand in mine and began to sing to her, however, the shaking instantly stopped and her body was calm and relaxed for the duration of the song."

*Performing for over 8 years*
**DAY JOB:** Elvis Tribute Artist
**HOME BASE:** Regina, Saskatchewan, Canada

# Janny James

"I recall performing in Chicago to an audience of 1,000 fans. I'd just started to sing 'Are You Lonesome Tonight', a real favorite of mine. I was shocked (as were the band and the female members of the audience) when all, yes, all of the men got up from their seats and made their way to the stage for a scarf and a kiss."

*Performing for over 10 years*
**DAY JOB:** Jockey
**HOME BASE:** Hertfordshire, England

# Ralph Elizondo

## "Tribute to Elvis"

"I am a spiritual guy (and I think Elvis was too). I personally feel that God uses people as vessels to bless others around the world. I receive God's blessings whenever I watch an Elvis movie or listen to his songs. The blessings are LAUGHTER and JOY. So you see, Elvis had a ministry and it changed my life."

*Performing for over 8 years*

**DAY JOB:** Elvis Tribute Artist **HOME BASE:** Houston, Texas

# Ray Covey

Ray has no trouble impersonating 'The King,' even though he has hearing loss in both ears. He manages a hearing aid service.

*Performing for over 11 years*

**DAY JOB:** Manager hearing aid service

**HOME BASE:** LaPorte, Texas

# Joe Tirrito

## "Tribute to 'The King'"

### The Friend I Never Knew

Now that he has said goodbye
Lord take him in your arms
The memories he left behind
Will linger for all times
That southern style
That half a smile
That shiny black hair
The way he moved in his early days
When no one else would dare
The happiness he gave to us
He now will give to you
Take good care of him dear Lord
My friend I never knew

His music brightened up our day
And touched our very world
And to us he'll always be
The King of Rock and Roll
So sing it tender, and sing it loud
And sing it, oh, so true
For now you'll sing
For the greatest King
Oh, Elvis we'll miss you
There will never be a performer
That's quite as great as you
But I'll carry on your legacy
My friend I never knew"

*Performing for over 20 years*

**DAY JOB:** Elvis Tribute Artist  **HOME BASE:** Countryside, Illinois

# Johnny Thompson

## "The King of Las Vegas"

"When doing a show at an Elvis night, I was performing a post-game concert to about 5,000 fans. As I was singing my last song of the night, 300 women chanting "Elvis" rushed the stage, yanked me off my feet and pulled me into the audience. It took 10 security guards to get through the women who were kissing me and pulling at me and trying to take a piece of me home. I was booked there again the next two years."

*Performing for over 10 years*

**DAY JOB:** Elvis Tribute Artist   **HOME BASE:** Las Vegas, Nevada

# Rick Ardisano

"Impersonators should feel honored that they can do Elvis."

*Performing for over 25 years*
**DAY JOB:** Printing Industry
**HOME BASE:** River Grove, Illinois

# Joey Franklin

## "A Touch of Elvis"

"The Lord gave me the voice.
I'm just using it."

Performing for over 5 years
**Elvis Tribute Artist**
**Las Vegas, Nevada**

# Randy Friskie

## "Viva Las Vegas"

"I prefer to think of myself
as someone performing a
tribute to the greatest
performer that ever lived."

*Performing for over 20 years*

**DAY JOB:** Elvis Tribute Artist

**HOME BASE:** Abbotsford, British Columbia, Canada

# Darren Lee

"I know there are a lot of Elvises out there who are trying to get my job."

Performing for over 15 years

**DAY JOB:** Elvis Tribute Artist
**HOME BASE:** Las Vegas, Nevada

# Jim Barone

## "A Tribute to Elvis"

"A woman named Rose, who was 89, came to see my show. She was around when Elvis first started playing. Rose enjoyed my show so much that each year she made her family celebrate her birthday with me. She celebrated with us into her mid-90s. All I can say is, 'God bless Rose.'"

*Performing for over 15 years*

**DAY JOB:** Elvis Tribute Artist
**HOME BASE:** Westfield, New Jersey

# Eddie Powers

"What are all these guys doing impersonating me?"

*Performing for over 15 years*

**DAY JOB:** Elvis Tribute Artist   **HOME BASE:** Las Vegas, Nevada

# Danny Dale

## "Elvis Memories Relived"

"The Elvis world is like a giant brotherhood or family. We all know each other, call each other on holidays, and when we travel, we get together and make chili." Danny actually has his own big family that performs. His wife, Norma Jean, impersonates Loretta Lynn and Tammy Wynette; his son, "Lil' D" does the young Elvis, and his other son does a tribute to a variety of country singers.

*Performing for over 4 years*

**DAY JOB:** Elvis Tribute Artist

**HOME BASE:** Louisville, Kentucky

# Kjell Bjornestad

"He is one of the few and gifted performers that has "it." He is like a firework on stage, with charisma and radiance in his possession. He is like a magnet to the audience and the media." — a fan

*Performing for over 17 years*
**DAY JOB:** Elvis Tribute Artist
**HOME BASE:** Lyngdal, Norway

# Michael Dean

## "Michael Dean and Memphis"

"I stood on top of a houseboat at the Decatur boat harbor and sang two songs in a $250 outfit I had made. Someone at the party booked us for another one and the act just mushroomed. The next thing I knew, I was buying $4,000 jumpsuits and singing all over the place."

Performing for over 9 years

**DAY JOB:** Elvis Tribute Artist

**HOME BASE:** Decatur, Alabama

# Ronny Craig

Ronny is now the best Elvis emcee out there because of his own experience as an Elvis performer. About Elvises: "You have to give them credit, because these guys put on the suit, put on the hair, and sing a tribute to the man they love."

*Performing for over 10 years*

**DAY JOB:** Entertainer and Elvis emcee

**HOME BASE:** LaCrosse, Wisconsin

# E Team Skydivers

## "The E Team Elvises of the Sky"

"Not to be confused with another set of skydivers who also have Elvis outfits, these guys put on quite a show whether lighting up the sky or the ground."

*Performing for over 30 years*

**DAY JOB:** Skydivers
**HOME BASE:** Mason, Ohio

# Kerry Summers

## "A Tribute to 'The King'"

"Jonathan, my little puppet guy, is the reason I'm doing an Elvis show in the first place. I started off as a ventriloquist and had much success. Using the puppet, I did different celebrity impersonations. One of the things I used to do was to put sideburns on him and let him sing an Elvis song. I worked very hard trying to master Elvis' singing voice and discovered that I had a natural, God-given gift when I sang."

*Performing for over 20 years*

**DAY JOB:** Entertainer

**HOME BASE:** Orem, Utah

# Eric Erikson

Eric has entertained as Elvis, and playing gospel music, ever since he was in the armed forces as a young man. "Elvis will never die as long as the Elvis Tribute Artists carry on his spirit. If I can be an inspiration to a younger generation, I will gladly do that."

*Performing for over 30 years*

**DAY JOB:** Entertainer  **HOME BASE:** Arcadia, Florida

# Charles King

"Performing as Elvis gives me many opportunities that no lawyer or doctor will ever have. Every year I perform for a non-profit group for children with AIDS. The most meaningful experience I've ever had was when a parent wrote to me and told me her daughter's last six months were happier because of the Elvis show, and how she wouldn't stop talking about how Elvis had sung to her."

Performing for over 12 years

**DAY JOB:** Elvis Tribute Artist

**HOME BASE:** Denver, Colorado

# Ed Parzygnat

*Performing for over 13 years*

**DAY JOB:** Entertainer
**HOME BASE:** Chicago, Illinois

# Yoshi Suzuki

Yoshi first learned how to speak English by listening to Elvis and imitating him. He was discovered on "The Gong Show," which led to him appearing in *Honeymoon in Vegas.*

*Performing for over 10 years*

**DAY JOB:** Photographer

**HOME BASE:** New York, New York

# Ginger Gilmore

## "Tribute To Elvis Presley"

"I have always been very much in love with Elvis. I used to be a professional boxer and he has been like a guardian

angel for me. He has gotten' me through tough times and taught me how to sing. Music is my life and Elvis is always a part of it."

*Performing for over 5 years*

**DAY JOB:** Entertainer

**HOME BASE:** Minneapolis, Minnesota

# Mark Hussman
## "Elvis Spectacular"

"Of all the roles I've done in my life, Elvis is the most complex. I did Hamlet in a Northwestern University acting class, and Elvis is harder than Hamlet. The golden rule question for me before going on stage is, 'Would Elvis appreciate what I am presenting?' Elvis' approval is key."

*Performing for over 10 years*
**DAY JOB:** Elvis Tribute Artist
**HOME BASE:** Chicago, Illinois

# Irv Cass

"Raise your glasses. Let's have a toast to Elvis. Let's have another toast to you, and raise your glasses again, because what I know and the other performers know, is the more you drink, the more we look and sound like Elvis."

*Performing for over 10 years*

**DAY JOB:** Elvis Tribute Artist    **HOME BASE:** Niles, Michigan

# Ray Guillemette Jr.

## "A Ray of Elvis"

Ray's determination is not only a tribute to Elvis, but a tribute to life. In 2001, he was hit by a drunk driver while on his motorcycle, and lost a leg. He has overcome this huge obstacle with a prosthetic leg and continues to triumph as a great Elvis performer.

*Performing for over 15 years*

**DAY JOB:** Elvis Tribute Artist

**HOME BASE:** Chicopee, Massachusetts

# Jay Allan

## "Tribute to Young Elvis"

"My career so far has been amazing and I thank God and Elvis for opening the door for me. My experiences are way too many to list, but one thing I know is I make a lot of people happy and they make me happy in return so that's a good thing. I have come across friends and relatives of Elvis who have told me, 'you're one guy that does remind me of Elvis.' That really touches me because I am a fan first and foremost. I plan to keep TCB for years to come!"

*Performing for over 10 years*

**DAY JOB:** Elvis Tribute Artist    **HOME BASE:** Bethlehem, Pennsylvania

# Steve Chappell

*Although Steve is normally very shy, when he is on stage he is the opposite! He jumps on tables, sings, dances and has great charisma. He does not try to look exactly like Elvis, as he keeps his own hair natural. "My show is for music and memories, not to make fun of somebody's looks. I don't do it for money, to pick up women, or for popularity. There is no need to do something if it's not wanted. I do it because the public asks."*

*Performing for over 10 years*

**DAY JOB:** Elvis Tribute Artist

**HOME BASE:** Augusta, Georgia

# Travis Morris

## "An American Trilogy"

Travis started out as an actor at Steppenwolf Theater in Chicago singing as Elvis, and ended up singing and entertaining as Elvis full-time.

Performing for over 12 years

**DAY JOB:** Elvis Tribute Artist

**HOME BASE:** Winthrop Harbor, Illinois

# Bill Henderson

"The Elvis tradition is flexible. It stretches or contracts to accommodate almost anyone who wants to give it a try." When not fronting his Elvis band, novelist Bill Henderson was a professor at North Carolina State University. His novel, *Stark Raving Elvis* and memoir, *I Elvis: Confessions of a Counterfeit King*, are classics of Elvis-inspired literature.

*Performing for over 8 years*

**DAY JOB:** Novelist
**HOME BASE:** Chapel Hill, North Carolina

# Rick Dunham

"Elvis Tribute Show"

"I like to move, but many of my moves don't look like Elvis. I do better when I don't concentrate on it too much and just try to have a good time. Being an Elvis Tribute Artist and performing almost every week for the past twenty years has changed my life. My strongest connection has been through baseball and many of my out-of-state shows have been in minor league baseball stadiums."

**DAY JOB:** Elvis Tribute Artist and Actor
**HOME BASE:** Springfield, Illinois

# David Moore

"The Heart of Elvis"

*Coincidences and Connections between Elvis and David Jesse Moore*

| Elvis | David |
|-------|-------|
| English-Irish-Cherokee | English-Irish-German-Cherokee |
| Born in Tupelo | Born in Tampa |
| Born in January | Born in January |
| Lived in Memphis | Lived in Molalla |
| Wife was Priscilla | Wife is Peggy |
| Shoe size: 12D | Shoe size: 12D |
| Called his baby "Buttonhead" | Called his baby "Butttonhead" |
| Father died on June 26 | Father-in-law was born on June 26 |
| High school mascots were the Lions | High school mascots were the Lions |
| Born near Highway 51 | Born near Highway 51 |

*Performing for over 15 years*

**DAY JOB:** Elvis Tribute Artist  **HOME BASE:** Mollala, Oregon

# Matt King

"The Profile of 'The King'"

*Performing for over 12 years*

**DAY JOB:** Elvis Tribute Artist

**HOME BASE:** Leslie, Michigan

# Justin Kurtis

"I was working at Elvis-A-Rama in the gift shop when one day I filled in for the regular Elvis performer, and here I am today!"

*Performing for over 2 years*
**DAY JOB:** Elvis Tribute Artist
**HOME BASE:** Las Vegas, Nevada

# Prentice Chaffin

## "Elvises of the Sky"

"I've been about everything from truck driver to inspector on nuclear reactors. Now I'm a truck mechanic. I believe I can sing Elvis as well or better than anyone I've ever heard. I always try to do it with class."

*Performing for over 10 years*

**DAY JOB:** Truck mechanic

**HOME BASE:** Columbus, Ohio

# Elvis Jr.

## "Memories Of 'The King'"

"When I was in Memphis for the first time in 1996, I realized that I will never meet my idol. The only way for me to be close to him is to be on stage!"

*Performing for over 8 years*

**DAY JOB:** Elvis Tribute Artist
**HOME BASE:** La Louviere, Belgium

# Kathy Ohsawa

*Performing for over 10 years*

**DAY JOB:** Entertainer
**HOME BASE:** Kumamoto, Japan

# Chris Solano

"I remember as a lonely 10-year-old boy, I would sing his songs of love. When I needed to feel uplifted, I would sing an upbeat song. I found Elvis' music to be both comforting and therapeutic, and after I watched his movies, he became my first real hero."

*Performing for over 5 years*

**DAY JOB:** Elvis Tribute Artist

**HOME BASE:** Ann Arbor, Michigan

# Leo Days

## "In Honor of Elvis"

"I love what I do and hope you all do too!"

*Performing for over 9 years*

**DAY JOB:** Elvis Tribute Artist and student    **HOME BASE:** Flint, Michigan

# Rick Marino

"You don't start out trying to be an Elvis impersonator. It is a career that finds you." Rick is THE expert on Elvis as a career, and has written an excellent book called, Be Elvis! A Guide to Impersonating the King. About a group of ETAs he commented, "All of us looked a little like Elvis but none of us looked like each other."

**DAY JOB:** Elvis Tribute Artist
**HOME BASE:** Jacksonville, Florida

# Patty Manning

*Performing for over 7 years*

**DAY JOB:** Painter
**HOME BASE:** Chicago, Illinois

# Jerome Marion

"It's a hard life with a lot of hours of work, rehearsals, private shows, and working most weekends. It can really take its toll on a relationship. But when you get on stage and the audience goes crazy, it seems worth it."

*Performing for over 14 years*

**DAY JOB:** Elvis Tribute Artist
**HOME BASE:** Tinley Park, Illinois

# Tony Grova

## "Memories of Elvis"

"There have been many kings and queens and presidents too, but never again in this lifetime or any lifetime to come, will there ever be another man or another entertainer as the one and only *Elvis Aaron Presley.*"

*Performing for over 25 years*

**DAY JOB:** Elvis Tribute Artist
**HOME BASE:** Ringwood, New Jersey

# Tony Rome

"I keep performing Elvis shows to keep people reminded of 'The King.' I think Elvis fans are the most wonderful people in the world. I do it for the smiles."

*Performing for over 30 years*
**DAY JOB:** Elvis Tribute Artist
**HOME BASE:** Cicero, Illinois

# Bob West

## "A Legend Lives On"

"Bob is the epitome of what Elvis would have wanted in a tribute artist." – a fan

*Performing for over 30 years*

**DAY JOB:** Municipal Supervisor
**HOME BASE:** Palos Hills, Illinois

# Dave Ehlert

## "Elvis and the Superstars Show"

"What drives an otherwise average baby boomer to end up in a backstage dressing room surrounded by bottles of hairspray, high-collared jumpsuits, and Brut cologne?" This is the enigmatic question that Dave Ehlert explains in his forthcoming memoir: *I Walked A Mile In His Shoes*. Dave has been performing in Elvis mode for over 30 years. As an interviewer recently put it, "You've been Elvis longer than Elvis was Elvis!"

*Performing for over 30 years*

**DAY JOB:** Elvis Tribute Artist    **HOME BASE:** Branson, Missouri

# Dwight Icenhower

## "Tribute to 'The King'"

"I'm a younger Elvis fan myself at only 20, and I have always regretted not being around to see 'The King' live and in person. Dwight's voice was amazing. It sounded so much like Elvis' that I had to tell myself, 'It's only an impersonator' over and over again. Thank you, Dwight, for helping me to come as close to a lifelong dream as I will ever be able to get—a trip back in time to see 'The King.' You rock!"
—a fan

*Performing for over 5 years*
**DAY JOB:** Elvis Tribute Artist
**HOME BASE:** Dexter, Ohio

# Billy Morokawa

Rock-a-Billy is an avid Elvis fan. He has been on Japanese television and won Elvis trivia contests. He is also a performer who has cut CDs at Sun Studios.

*Performing for over 15 years*
**DAY JOB:** Elvis Tribute Artist
**HOME BASE:** Tokyo, Japan

# Brendan Paul

## "Have Sideburns Will Travel"

The owner of Graceland Wedding Chapel, and standing 6'4" without hair (6'7" with hair), Brendan has a great sense of humor while maintaining a professional demeanor. "Everyone mourned Elvis when he died, but for me it created a job opportunity! I'll be out of work if he comes back!"

*Performing for over 8 years*
**DAY JOB:** Elvis Tribute Artist
**HOME BASE:** Las Vegas, Nevada

# Robert Washington

"You know I'm not original, but I am different." Robert Washington is a family man, a great performer and a gentleman, who is totally unique. He performs a fantastic athletic Elvis performance, yet maintains his cool and his sweet nature. The man is a king among other ETAs.

*Performing for over 15 years*
**DAY JOB:** Painter
**HOME BASE:** Auburn, Maine

# Tim Welch

"I am here to give you some Elvis, but I am not him."

*Performing for over 10 years*
**DAY JOB:** Elvis Tribute Artist
**HOME BASE:** Las Vegas, Nevada

# Walt Sanders

## "A Tribute to Elvis© Like None Other"

"A lady came up to me and shook my hand and said, 'My God, I have seen Elvis two times and you have really got him down. You're different, you're not like all those other guys...you're real.'"

Walt opens his shows with, "Good evening Ladies and Gentlemen, I'm Kurt Russell!"

*Performing for over 10 years*
**DAY JOB:** Elvis Tribute Artist
**HOME BASE:** Bellevue, Ohio

# Elvez

"I'm not an Elvis impersonator, I'm an Elvis translator."

"Think globally act Elvisly."

"I'm a cross cultural caped crusader for truth, justice,
and the Mexican-American way."

"If Elvis grew up listening to Santana and Stray Cats he'd be Elvez."

"You too can be King."

*Performing for over 20 years*

**DAY JOB:** Entertainer  **HOME BASE:** Seattle, Washington

# Don Romines

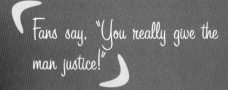

Fans say, "You really give the man justice!"

*Performing for over 17 years*
**DAY JOB:** Engineer  **HOME BASE:** Schenectady, New York

# Dennis Stella

*A female fan who had met him for the first time commented, "What a neat guy and great pecs!"*

*Performing for over 12 years*
**DAY JOB:** Insurance salesman
**HOME BASE:** Chicago, Illinois

# Don and Ryan Rose

## "The Don Rose Revue"

"Estelle Brown, one of the Sweet Inspirations who backed up Elvis, said to me, 'Elvis would have loved to sit and listen to you sing!" Although most kids want to watch Sesame Street, little Ryan Rose wants to watch his daddy. His own dream came true when he asked Santa for his own Elvis jumpsuit. Since Santa is no slouch, he got Ryan a professional one to match Daddy Don's!

*Performing for over 20 years*
**DAY JOB:** Elvis Tribute Artist
**HOME BASE:** Las Vegas, Nevada

# Fred Wolfe

## "Voice of 'The King'"

"I attract a lot of women doing Elvis, but they are never the right ones! The perks are the nice things people do for you because of what you do for them. Having black hair and sideburns really breaks the ice."

*Performing for over 15 years*

**DAY JOB:** Elvis Tribute Artist

**HOME BASE:** Royal Oak, Michigan

# Gene Shaw

## "Memories of Elvis"

"I came up in the 50s as a teenager when Elvis was getting started. I have loved Elvis and his music all my life. I have been teased about looking like Elvis for about 35 years. I feel that Elvis gave the world the best voice and entertainment that the world has ever known. I am referred to as 'Elvis' everywhere I go."

*Performing for over 30 years*

**DAY JOB:** Elvis Tribute Artist

**HOME BASE:** Monroe, Louisiana

# Stephen Kabakos

## "The Way It Was"

*Performing for over 10 years*

**DAY JOB:** Elvis Tribute Artist
**HOME BASE:** Milton, Ontario, Canada

# Doug Church

## "The Voice of Elvis"

"If I wasn't doing what I am doing now, I would be wishing I was doing what I am doing now."

"Don't do unto others if they haven't done unto you cause you might get done in doing it!"

*Performing for over 20 years*
**DAY JOB:** Elvis Tribute Artist    **HOME BASE:** Mishawaka, Indiana

# Michael Vegas

## "The Michael Vegas Show"

*"What a wonderful show again as usual! I believe Elvis' spirit enters your body somehow...Its amazing."* —a fan

*Performing for over 7 years*
**DAY JOB:** Elvis Tribute Artist
**HOME BASE:** Yorktown Heights, New York

# Dean Z

"The thing I love the most is when some little kid comes up to me after a show and tells me that 'because of you I am now an Elvis fan.'"

*Performing for over 10 years*
**DAY JOB:** Elvis Tribute Artist
**HOME BASE:** Lancaster, California

# Yasumasa Mori

"I am definitely not a look-alike because you can always put on makeup and sideburns to look like him; I wanted to be him. I wanted to express who he was using my own voice, feelings, actions and passion."

*Performing for over 15 years*
**DAY JOB:** Elvis Tribute Artist
**HOME BASE:** Tokyo, Japan

# John Loos

## "The Sounds of Elvis"

"John, any word that explains your performances is an understatement. Exciting, amazing, phenomenal: nothing cuts it. The first time I saw you live was when I was 10; I am 15 now. I thought you were amazing then, and you've gotten even better since. I can't get over how great your voice is, your moves, your sex appeal, your charisma— EVERYTHING." – a fan

*Performing for over 5 years*

**DAY JOB:** Elvis Tribute Artist
**HOME BASE:** Cheyenne, Wyoming

# *Afterword*
## by Bill Henderson

y questionable career as an Elvis impersonator took a quantum leap the day I met Patty Carroll, and I'm sure I'm not alone in feeling that way. Because Patty—visionary artist, consummate pro, holder of prestigious teaching positions in England and America—was our Cecil Beaton, Annie Leibowitz, or Richard Avedon. Those, of course, are not the terms impresario Doc Franklin used to describe her on the phone, when I called him in Memphis to explain a book project and beg for a pass into his Images of Elvis Contest, the granddaddy of all such events—and the World Series for Elvis impersonators. "There's a girl comes back here every year snapping pictures. I let her set up in a room behind the stage." Strictly true, maybe. It was in fact a room behind the stage. But Patty and an assistant had transformed it into a fully functioning portrait studio, complete with lighting, a seamless white backdrop, and a variety of state-of-the-art portrait cameras. And you could hardly call what she did "snapping pictures." Each Elvis got a full photo shoot the likes of which he probably never saw again.

From behind her camera, Patty led each performer through his paces, with a confidence born of much experience in how to coax into being the essence of whatever she saw in a subject.

It's through the photos that came out of my session that I first began (rightly or wrongly) to feel "authentic." I'm sure there are a few excellent impersonators somewhere who have not been photographed by Patty, but the fact remains that her distinctive style made legitimate icons out of more than one run-of-the-mill Elvis.

To this day I look at my Patty Carroll portfolio (one of her photos became the cover of my book, *I Elvis, Confessions of a Counterfeit King*) to remind myself that yes, I once did this—and to judge from those pictures, it's possible—I wasn't half bad.

So thank you, Patty. I and several hundred other Elvis impersonators owe you a great debt. In this crazy world where everyone chases the image, you made us real.

# Thank you, thank you very much.

by Patty Carroll

This project has been a true labor of love, from loving Elvis and his world, to my husband who has put up with many weeks of me trotting around the country in pursuit of a few more pictures. I would like to officially thank Tony Jones, my supportive husband, for his patience and fortitude while I pursued my photographic projects, this one being the most time consuming and outrageous of many of them! I would also like to thank all of the great people that have been so helpful to me while making these pictures.

In Memphis, Doc and Jackie Franklin became friends and lent rooms at their competitions in which to photograph the Elvises. Maurice Curet, my late friend known as Frenchy, kept me shored up and full of coffee when I was down. The various assistants who accompanied me on these journeys of love and labor: Kelly Costello, Suky Best, Jonine Pietroski, Michele Giffune, Maribeth Carroll and all the rest of the teams that worked with me. A special thanks also to Ben Fink, who let me use his studio in Memphis, and put us up and put up with us while often in Memphis! Also a thanks to Jeff Niesan and the staff at Memphis College of Art for their participation and exhibition opportunity.

In the Chicago and Indiana area, so many thanks to Nance Fox and the Elvis Entertainers Network for their support and help in letting me photograph at events.

A thank you to Dan Lentino of Ambassador Talent Services, and a thanks to Mark Hussman, an ETA, who organizes events and who has helped me out at various opportunities, and always let me photograph at his extravaganzas. Caroline Nelson has been my helper and office organizer throughout the production of the book, and is also greatly appreciated.

Recently in Las Vegas, thanks to the photography team from Photographers on the Fly, especially Mark, George and Gina. A special thank you to Cupid's Wedding Chapel for the use of their studio, as well as Graceland Wedding Chapel. A huge thanks to Kristy Royle, for setting me up with many performers and the photo team in Las Vegas. She has been a royal dream to work with! She also gave me suggestions and support during the making of this book.

A huge, big thanks to Gary Chassman at Verve Editions, who has shown great patience and resolve in producing this book, his able assistant Eliza Shanley, and our phenomenal designer, Stacey Hood at Big Eyedea Visual Design. This team is the best I have ever seen for book packaging and production!

Most importantly, thank you to all of the Elvis Tribute Artists who have participated in this project. Not all of them made it into the book, but all of them were great!

I apologize to those whose pictures do not appear here, but we had to make decisions based on all kinds of factors, most of all to make a great book that features the work, love and devotion of all Elvis performers and fans.

# Contact information

**Mike Albert**
Website: www.mikealbertsings.com
Email:
UltimateTribute@mikealbertsings.com

**Peter Alden**
Website:
peteraldenfanclub.tripod.com/index.html
Email: fauxep@hotmail.com

**Jay Allan**
Website:
members.aol.com/fever999/index.html
Email: JayAllanRocks@aol.com

**Rory Allen**
Website: www.roryallen.com
Email: rory@roryallen.com

**Rick Ardisano**
Contact: Sally Verity, Tel: 708-456-1011

**Johnny Baron**
Website: www.classiqueproductions.com/
pages/PAGE526L.HTM
Email: classique2@cox.net

**Jim Barone**
Website: www.jimbarone.com
Email: jimbarone@jimbarone.com

**Shawn Barry**
Website:
www.shawnbarryentertainment.com
Email: info@shawnbarryentertainment.com

**Kjell Bjornestad**
Website: www.elvis.no
Email: re-entertainment@elvis.no

**Gene Capaul**
Email: gcapaul@hotmail.com

**Irv Cass**
Website: www.irvcass.com
www.elvisentertainersonline.com/
entertainers/Irv_Cass
Email: keesullivan@hotmail.com
een@elvisentertainersonline.com

**Prentice Chaffin**
Website: www.prenticechaffin.com/
Email: chaffin865@aol.com

**Steve Chappell**
Website: members.aol.com/schappell1
Email: schappell3@aol.com

**Doug Church**
Website: www.dougchurchusa.com
Email: doug@dougchurchusa.com

**Ray Covey**
Website: www.texaselvisexplosion.com/
raycovey.htm
Email: ELVISbyray@hotmail.com

**Ronny Craig**
Website: www.elvisentertainersonline.com/
entertainers/Ronny_Craig/index.html
Email: een@elvisentertainersonline.com

**Danny Dale (Danny Shouse)**
Website: www.dannydaletcb.com/
www.elvisentertainersonline.com/
entertainers/Danny_Dale/
Email: ElvisMemories@bellsouth.net

**Leo Days**
Website: www.ledpro.homestead.com
www.leodays.com
Email: ledpro@comcast.net

**Michael Dean**
Website: www.michaeldeanandmemphis.com
www.elvisentertainersonline.com/
entertainers/Michael_Dean
Email: rmichaeldean@cs.com

**Rick Dunham**
Website: elvishimselvis.tripod.com
Email: elvisdunham77@hotmail.com

**Donny Edwards**
Website: www.donnyedwards.com
www.royaltalent.com
Email: royalbooking@aol.com

**Dave Ehlert**
Website: www.elvisinbranson.com
Email: daveelvisehlert@yahoo.com

**E Team Skydivers**
Paul McCowan Airshows
Website: www.eteamskydivers.com/
Email: paulmccowan@eteamskydivers.com

**Ralph Elizondo**
Website: www.houstonelvis.com/
www.elvisentertainersonline.com/
entertainers/Ralph_Elizondo/
Email: ralphelizondo@msn.com

**Elvez (Robert Lopez)**
Website: www.elvez.net
Email: elvezco@aol.com

**Eric Erikson**
Website: www.elvisentertainersonline.com/
entertainers/Eric_Erickson/index.html
Email: een@elvisentertainersonline.com
erikson@strato.net

**Joey Franklin**
Email: atouchofelvis@aol.com

**Randy Friskie**
Website: www.randyelvisfriskie.com
Email: info@randyelvisfriskie.com

**Ginger Gilmore**
Website: www.rar2000enterprise.com/
elvisgingergilmore1/
Email: elvisginger@yahoo.com

**Tony Grova**
Website: www.tonygrova.com
Email: tony@tonygrova.com

**Ray Guillemette Jr.**
Website: www.arayofelvis.com/

**Bill Henderson**
Website: williammccranorhenderson.com/
www.applestocknation.com/
billhendersoncopy.com/
Email: wmhenderson@nc.rr.com

**Michael Hoover**
Website: www.michaelhoover.com

**Mark Hussman**
Website: www.markelvis.com
Email: MarkElvis@aol.com

**Dwight Icenhower**
Website: www.dwighticenhower.com
www.elvisentertainersonline.com/
entertainers/Dwight_Icenhower

**Janny James (Janis Waite)**
Website: janjames2000.tripod.com
Email: Jannyjames5@aol.com

**Elvis Jr. (Franck Elliaerts)**
Website: www.elvisjunior.com
Email: info@elvisjunior.com

**Stephen Kabakos**
Website: www.tvband.com
Email: tvbonlinemail@cogeco.ca

**Matt King**
Website: www.zyworld.com/MATTKING/
  bio_page.htm
www.elvisentertainer.com
www.elvisentertainersonline.com/
  entertainers/Matt_King/
Email: elvisforhire@hotmail.com
elvisofthe70s@yahoo.com

**Charles King (Charles Byrne)**
Website: www.elvislive.com
Email: charleskingep@yahoo.com
Charles@elvislive.com

**Justin Kurtis**
Website: www.justinkurtis.com
Email: j7777@cox.net

**Darren Lee**
Website: www.darren-lee.com

**John Loos**
Website: www.johnloos.4mg.com
Email: Orinloos@cs.com,
johnloos@rogers.com

**Patty Manning**
Website: pattyelvis.com
Email: mail@pattyelvis.com

**Rick Marino**
Website: hometown.aol.com/rickmarinotcb/
Email: rickmarinotcb@aol.com

**Jerome Marion**
Website: www.elvisentertainersonline.com/
  entertainers/Jerome_Marion/
www.celebrityimpressions.com/Lookalikes/
  Elvis/index.htm
Email: Celebrityimp@aol.com

**David Moore**
Website: www.heartofelvis.cjb.net
Email: 1elvis@agora.rdrop.com

**Yasumasa Mori (J'Elvis)**
Website: jelvis.cool.ne.jp/English%20New/
  indexe.htm
Email: dhch@interlinc.net

**Billy Morokawa**
Website: www.Billy-Morokawa.com/
Email: billy_rockabilly@yahoo.co.jp

**Travis Morris**
Website: www.elvisentertainersonline.com/
  entertainers/Travis_Morris
Email: een@elvisentertainersonline.com

**Kathy Ohsawa**
Website: www.kathy-osawa.com/
Email: songbird@kathy-osawa.com

**Ed Parzygnat (Monkey Man)**
Website: www.elvisentertainersonline.com/
  entertainers/Ed_Parzygnat/
Email: mnkysndmr@aol.com,
een@elvisentertainersonline.com

**Brendan Paul**
Website: www.bestelvis.com/
Email: Brendan@bestelvis.com

**Eddie Powers**
Website: www.bestelvisinvegas.com
Email: eddie@bestelvisinvegas.com

**Tony Rome**
Email: tonyromeelvis@yahoo.com

**Don Romines**
Email: donelvisrom@aol.com

**Don and Ryan Rose**
Website: www.alohafromlasvegas.com/
http://www.smashproductions.com/don/
  don.html
http://www.elvisentertainersonline.com/
  entertainers/Don_Rose
Email: DrElvis2000@yahoo.com

**Walt Sanders**
Website: www.onenightwithyou.net/
Email: ws_tcb_tribute@hotmail.com
wsanders@onenightwithyou.net

**Justin Shandor**
Website: www.justinshandor.com
Email: dlentino@wideopenwest.com

**Gene Shaw**
Phone: 318-32-ELVIS or 318-396-5194

**Steve Sogura**
Website: www.steve-elvis-sogura.com/
Email: shirley@sammamishescrow.com

**Chris Solano**
Website: www.alltribute.com/chrissolano
Email: etribute@hotmail.com

**Michael Vegas**
Website: www.michaelvegas.com
Email: Burninluv@aol.com
KingsFootsteps@aol.com

**Dennis Stella**
Website: www.elvisentertainersonline.com/
  entertainers/Dennis_Stella
Email: een@elvisentertainersonline.com
ditalstaln@msn.com

**Kerry Summers**
Website: www.kerrysummers.com
Email: kerryaselvis@yahoo.com

**Yoshi Suzuki (Robert Kim)**
Website: www.asianelvis.com
Email: suspiciousfans@aol.com

**Junior Talley**
Website: juniortalley.20fr.com/
Email: JUNIORTALLEY@frontier.net

**Joe Tirrito**
Website: www.joeelvistirrito.com
Email: joeelvistirrito@hotmail.com

**Johnny Thompson**
Website: www.johnny-thompson.com
Email: RoyalBooking@aol.com,
LasVegasFlash@aol.com

**Robert Washington**
Website: www.elvisentertainersonline.com/
  entertainers/Robert_Washington/
Email: adickkey@aol.com,
een@elvisentertainersonline.com

**Bob West**
Website: www.geocities.com/bobwestelvis/

**Tim Welch**
Website: www.timwelchaselvis.com
Email: info@timwelchaselvis.com

**Fred Wolfe**
Website: www.fredwolf.com
Email: voiceoftheking@wideopenwest.com

**Dean Z (Dean Zeligman)**
Website: www.deanz.com
Email: deanz@prodigy.net

*Living the Life: The World of Elvis Tribute Artists*

Library of Congress Cataloging-in-Publication Data available

10 9 8 7 6 5 4 3 2 1

ISBN 0-9660352-9-1

Manufactured in China

Concept and art direction Gary Chassman

Distributed by Verve Editions, Ltd

209 College Street
Burlington, Vermont 05401
www.verveeditions.com

Living the Life is available for quantity purchase at a volume discount.
Please contact verve@together.net for details.

A product of lunacy from
Living the Life, LLC
2505 West Chicago, Avenue
Chicago, Illinois 60622

For additional information about the photographs of
Patty Carroll please contact her at www.pattycarroll.com

Art direction and coordination Gary Chassman and Patty Carroll
Book design Stacey Hood, Big Eyedea Visual Design
Editorial coordination and editing Eliza Shanley
Production and editorial assistance Caroline Nelson